GLOBETROTTERS
FRANCE
Jane Hinche
I0760092
REDBACK
publishing

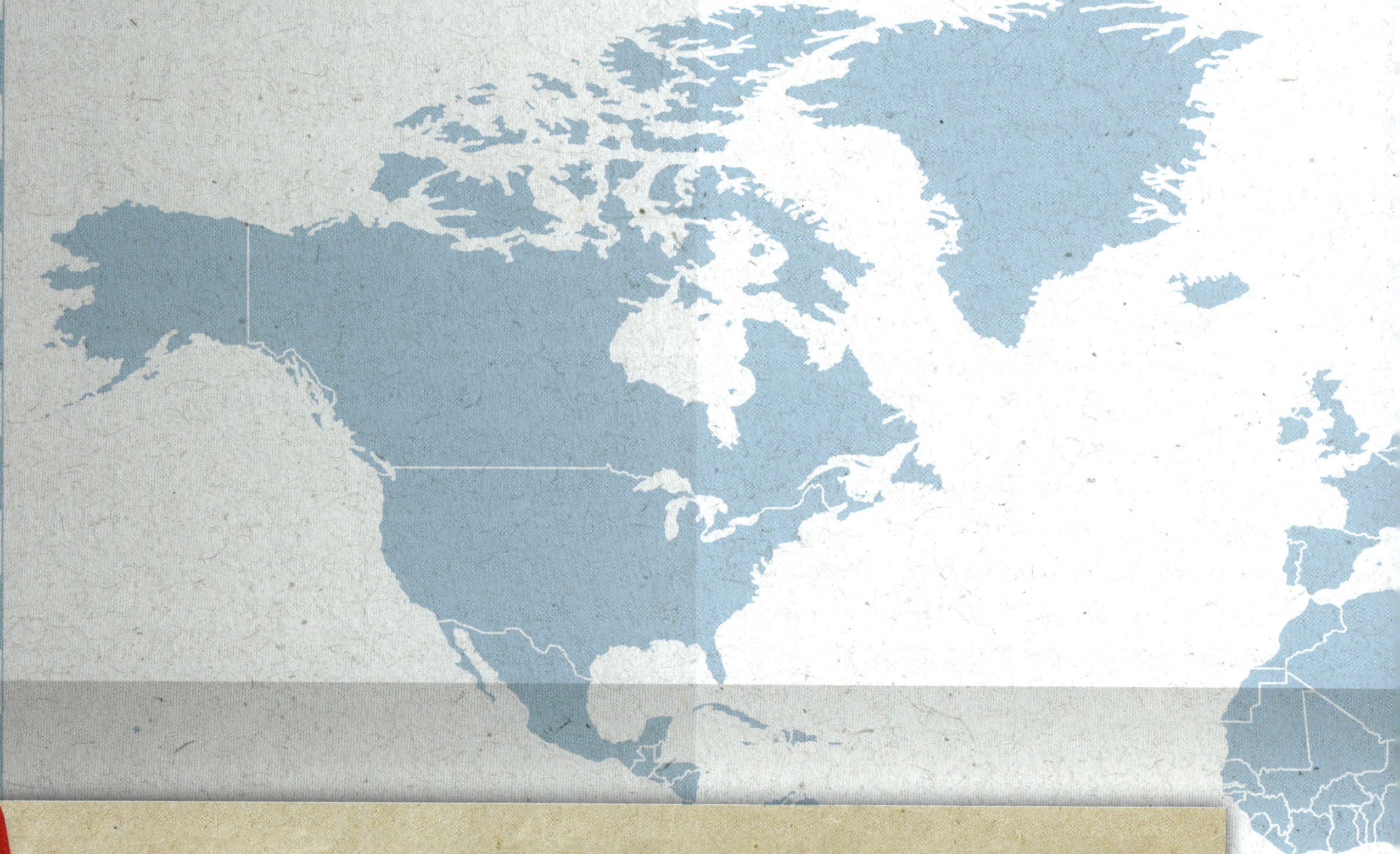

Redback Publishing
Suite 6, 13a Narabang Way,
Belrose NSW 2085
Australia

www.redbackpublishing.com
orders@redbackpublishing.com

ISBN 978-1-761401-45-9 PBK

Author: Jane Hinchey
Editor: Marlene Vaughan
Design: Redback Publishing

Original illustrations © Redback Publishing 2025
Originated by Redback Publishing

Acknowledgements
Abbreviations: l—left, r—right, b—bottom, t—top, c—centre, m—middle
We would like to thank the following for permission to reproduce photographs: (Images © shutterstock) p4bl catwalker, p5tl Nattee Chalermtiragool, p10tr Alexandra Lande, p11 tl Influential Photography, p11br Radu Razvan, p14tl antoniobarrosfr, p14tr FashionStock.com, p16tl Petr Kovalenkov, p16ml kavalenkava, p18bl DreamSlamStudio, p19tr Pykodelbi, p19b Kiev.Victor, p21tm Everett Historical, p21m By Jacques-Louis David, p24br olrat, p27br Netfalls Remy Musser, p28br andre quinou, p29tl thipjang, p30tr Frederic Legrand COMEO, p30m By Aimé Thomé de Gamond (1807-1876), p30br Dennis van de Water

Every effort has been made to contact copyright holders of any material reproduced in this book. Any omissions will be rectified in subsequent printings if notice is given to the publisher.

A catalogue record for this book is available from the National Library of Australia

CONTENTS

MAP OF FRANCE

FRANCE

IRELAND
ENGLAND
NETHERLANDS
BELGIUM
LUXEMBOURG

France

Rouen
Paris
Strasbourg
MONT SAINT-MICHEL
Rennes
Lyon
LASCAUX
Bordeaux
Grenoble
CHAMONIX
Toulouse
Marseille
ANDORRA
SPAIN
PALMA

Mont Saint Michel
MONT SAINT MICHEL

Prehistoric Cave Paintings
LASCAUX

Chamonix Mont Blanc
CHAMONIX

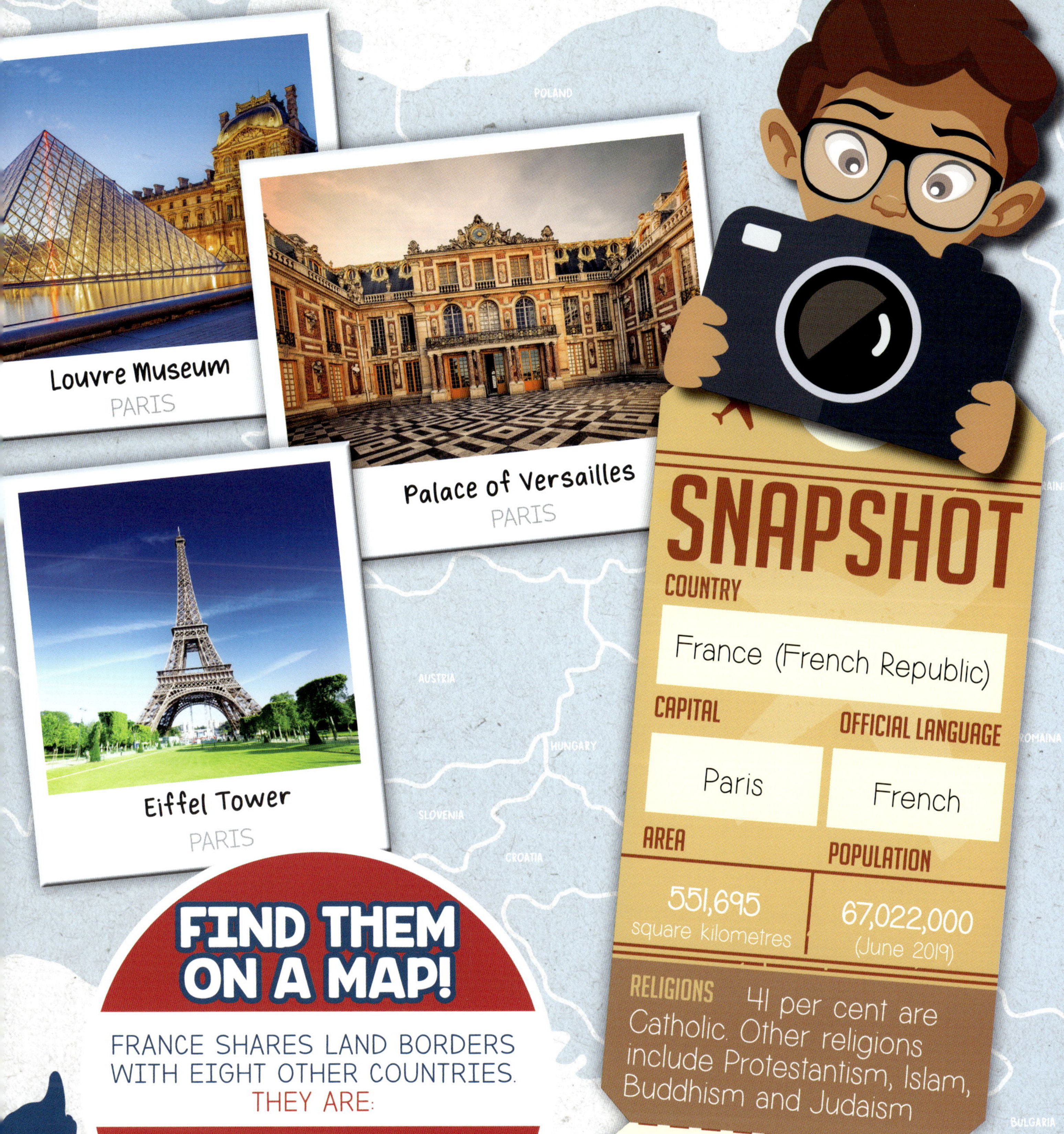

FIND THEM ON A MAP!

FRANCE SHARES LAND BORDERS WITH EIGHT OTHER COUNTRIES. THEY ARE:

- Spain
- Andorra
- Italy
- Switzerland
- Germany
- Monaco
- Luxembourg
- Belgium

SNAPSHOT

COUNTRY
France (French Republic)

CAPITAL
Paris

OFFICIAL LANGUAGE
French

AREA
551,695 square kilometres

POPULATION
67,022,000 (June 2019)

RELIGIONS 41 per cent are Catholic. Other religions include Protestantism, Islam, Buddhism and Judaism

CURRENCY
€ Euro

GOVERNMENT
France is a unitary semi-presidential republic

WELCOME TO FRANCE

France is the largest country in Western Europe, and the largest European country after Russia. It has been inhabited for tens of thousands of years. Prehistoric sites in southwest France indicate people have been in the region for at least 35,000 years.

Celtic tribes known as Gauls arrived around 1,000 BC and settled in the area until Julius Caesar conquered it in 50 BC. The Roman Empire then ruled for 500 years. After the fall of the Roman Empire, Germanic Francs dominated the region. The name 'France' originates from the term Francs.

Prehistoric drawing, representation of a bull
CAVE OF LASCAUX

Did You Know?

The national motto is ***Liberté, égalité, fraternité*** meaning 'liberty, equality, fraternity'.

Today France is one of the most important nations in the Western world. It is a republic, meaning its citizens elect a president as Head of State. It has a strong tradition of the arts and French people are known for their love of food and quality of life.

Top Imports

- Crude Petroleum
- Coffee
- Chocolate
- Fruit juice
- Tobacco

Top Exports

- Wheat
- Aluminium
- Refined petroleum
- Corn
- Barley

1,000,000,624

CHEESY BUT TRUE

France produces more than **one billion tons** of cheese each year and more than 1,000 different varieties.

1 BILLION TONS

PEOPLE

The French descend from many different cultural groups and peoples, including the Celts, Romans, Franks and Normans.

Pyrenees Mountains
SOUTHWEST FRANCE

Brittany is home to Bretons who are the ancestors of the Celts. The Breton language and Celtic traditions such as music are still strong in this region.

France is also home to many immigrant groups, whose customs have merged into the very fabric of French culture. In France there are between five to eight million people from Maghreb countries such as Algeria, Morocco and Tunisia. These people are called *Maghrebins* in France. Some Maghrebis were born in France but have Maghrebi parents who emigrated to the country.

There are also smaller communities of Jews, Romany people, Southeast Asians and people of other European backgrounds.

DAILY LIFE

Joie de vivre, which means 'a love of life' is important in France. This doesn't mean that everyone is happy all of the time, but the French do take pleasure in everyday life – they savour their leisure time and cultural pursuits.

Family is important and the French make time to dine together each day. On weekends, it's common for extended family to come together to share lunch or dinner.

The French get five weeks annual leave, and many of them take that over the summer. period

Depending on the region, there will be customs and traditions that are still practised today. Traditional dress still exists in some areas, although it is largely reserved for official ceremonies and festivals.

Good Manners!

Etiquette is highly regarded. In France, it's polite to greet people you meet in day-to-day circumstances, even if they are strangers.

Life in Towns and Cities

Residents living in towns and cities enjoy easy access to good bakeries, markets, delicatessens, cafes and restaurants. People play sport, visit galleries and museums and attend events. Families can choose from good school and medical facilities, and children have quite a lot of freedom and independence from a young age.

The Louvre Museum

PARIS

Rural Areas

Life hasn't changed much for generations in the French countryside, where community is important. Unlike many countries, there has been a shift towards moving from cities back to rural areas, which has helped maintain populations.

SPORT

The French love sport. Tennis, rugby, basketball, ice-hockey, handball and motor sports are all very popular. Skiing is also a popular winter pastime, but nothing can beat the country's two favourite sports: football and cycling.

Football

One of the most popular sports in France is football, with nearly two million licensed players. France won the FIFA World Cup in 1998 and in 2018.

The Tour De France

The Tour de France is an annual men's cycling road race that attracts hundreds of thousands of spectators each year. The first Tour de France was held in 1903 and had 15 competitors. Now, around 200 cyclists race over a three week period, travelling 3,600 kilometres and finishing in Paris.

EDUCATION

Did You Know?

Education in France is compulsory and free

Children attend school from age six to sixteen. The French take education very seriously, and school days can be long. There are different stages, from primary to secondary school, and then to *lycée*, where students study for the *baccalauréat* or do subjects that lead to work. All students who pass the *baccalauréat* can attend university.

Eat Up!

Each school day includes a long break of up to two hours for lunch. Students sit at tables and eat a balanced meal at the school canteen. The French government provides a freshly-prepared meal for over six million public school children each day. The meals include a starter, a main meal, dessert and a fruit snack. The meals are healthy, consisting of salad, vegetables, meat, fish and eggs.

Junk food has no place in the French school lunch.

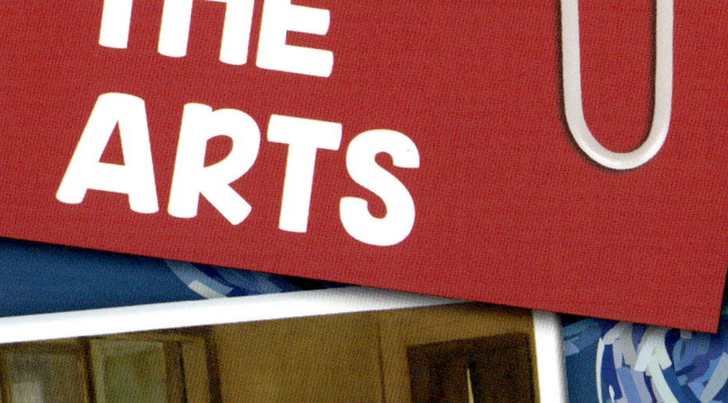

THE ARTS

France has produced many of the world's great artists, writers, painters and musicians. The French pride themselves on their artistic reputation and heritage.

First Impressions

Impressionism is a nineteenth century art movement, started by a group of artists in Paris. The group held its first exhibition in Paris in 1874, but people ridiculed the art. Time has proved the critics wrong and these artists continue to have their work viewed in galleries by millions of people each year.

Degas

Monet

Renoir

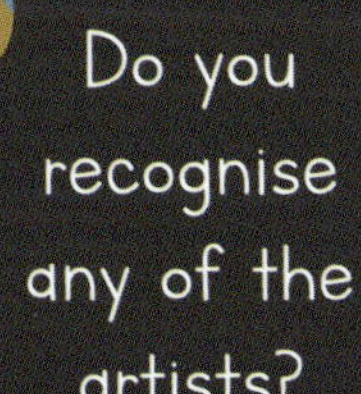

Do you recognise any of the artists?

Cezanne

Manet

On the Runway

Paris is the fashion capital of the world and home to designers such as Coco Chanel, Yves Saint Laurent, Jean-Paul Gaultier, Christian Dior, Hubert de Givenchy, and Christian Lacroix.

The Thinker

Rodin, a famous sculptor, created many revered works, but his most famous is *The Thinker*.

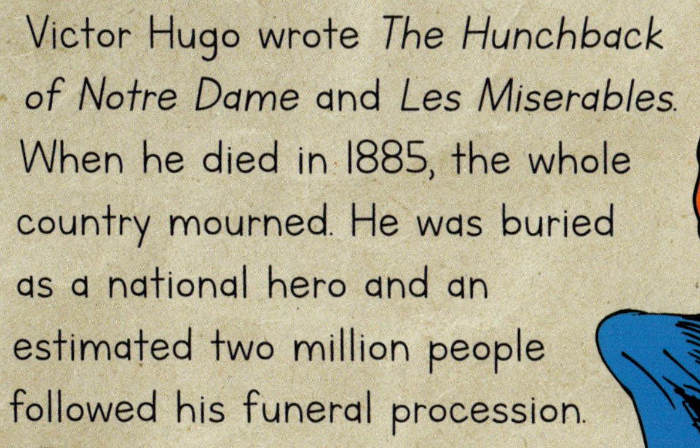

Victor Hugo wrote *The Hunchback of Notre Dame* and *Les Miserables*. When he died in 1885, the whole country mourned. He was buried as a national hero and an estimated two million people followed his funeral procession.

Did You Know?

French writers have won the Nobel Prize for Literature more than writers from any other country.

Famous Writers

France has produced many notable writers such as Voltaire, Proust and Moliere. Some famous books you may have heard of are:

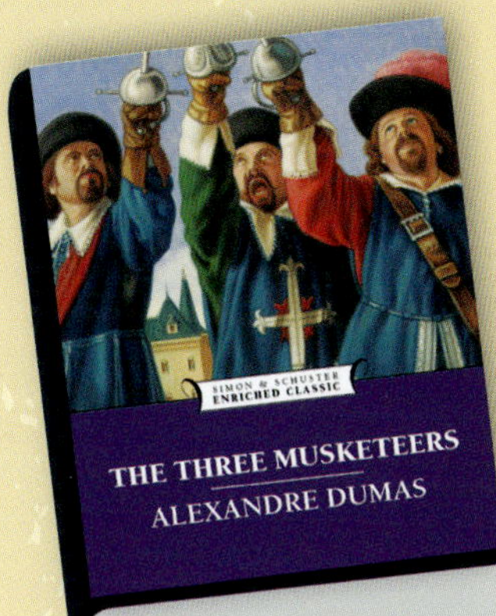

Two of the most famous cafes are La Rotonde and Les Deux Magots.

PARIS CAFES

Paris is full of cafes and bars where you can soak in the city's literary history. Traditionally, the coffee houses of Europe were meeting places for artists and intellectuals.

Gertrude Stein, F. Scott Fitzgerald, T. S. Eliot and Ernest Hemingway were all regulars at Cafe La Rotonde. Hemingway even wrote about it in *The Sun Also Rises*:

«No matter what cafe in Montparnasse you ask a taxi-driver to bring you to from the right bank of the river, they always take you to the Rotonde.»

Another Hemingway haunt, Les Deux Magots, one of the oldest cafes in Paris, is now a famous tourist spot. Other legendary writers who were patrons included Jean Nicolas Arthur Rimbaud, Simone de Beauvoir and Jean Paul Sartre.

LANGUAGE

Learn the Lingo

No
Non

Excuse Me
Excusez-moi

Good Night
Bonne nuit

Yes
Oui

Good Evening
Bonsoir

Thank You
Merci

PLEASE
S'il vous plait

Good Morning
Bonjour

The National language is French, which has its roots in Latin, as well as Gallic, Celtic, and Germanic languages. There are a number of different dialects around France, as well as some regional languages.

Did You Know?

French is spoken as a first or second language in 47 countries.

RELIGION AND HOLIDAYS

Over 63 per cent of France's population is Christian and the majority of those are Catholic. There are smaller communities of Protestants and Lutherans. Islam is the second most practised religion, with eight per cent of the population being Muslim. There are smaller Sikh and Jewish communities. Around 25 per cent of French people don't subscribe to any religion.

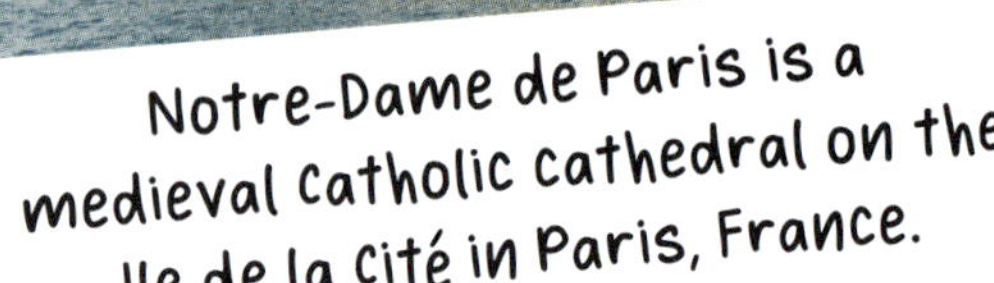

Notre-Dame de Paris is a medieval Catholic cathedral on the Ile de la Cité in Paris, France.

Holidays and Festivals

The French observe many public holidays throughout the year. The two regions of Alsace and Lorraine have two extra public holidays. Six of these public holidays are religious holidays according to the Christian calendar.

Bastille Day

France's national holiday is Bastille Day. The Bastille is a fortress in Paris that was used to imprison anyone who opposed the king. On July 14, 1789 the storming of the Bastille took place. This signalled the start of the French Revolution and the end of the Monarchy. Bastille Day is celebrated annually on July 14, with military parades and events all over the country.

Christmas

Christmas is an important religious celebration for French people. Families gather together on either Christmas Eve or Christmas Day

During the festive season, cities and towns are draped in decorations and lights and many hold annual Christmas markets. The markets are filled with stalls that sell artisan goods and foods such as sugar cookies and roasted chestnuts.

FRANCE TIMELINE

400 BC

Celtic tribes settle in the region

58 BC

Romans invade Gaul

52 BC

Julius Caesar conquers the region

768 – 814 AD

Charlemagne reigns

843 AD

The Frankish Empire is divided between Charlemagne's sons. These regions later become France and Germany

895 AD

Vikings settle in Normandy

1066

Duke William of Normandy conquers England

1337 – 1453

Hundred Years' War between France and England

1429

Joan of Arc, a peasant girl, leads the French to victory at the Siege of Orleans

1431

Joan of Arc is burned at the stake

1643 – 1715

The Sun King, Louis XIV, is King of France

1789 – 1792

The French Revolution - France becomes a Republic

1793

King Louis XVI and Marie Antoinette are executed by guillotine

1804

Napoleon crowns himself Emperor of France and controls much of Europe

1815

Napoleon is defeated at the Battle Waterloo

1889

The Eiffel Tower is built for the World's Fair

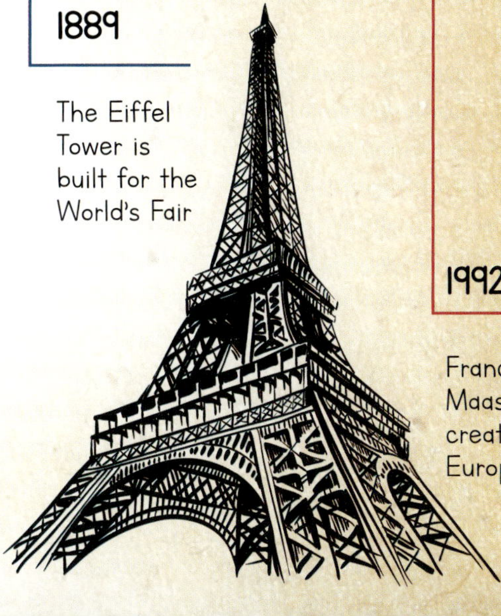

1914–1918

World War I
- 1.3 million French people are killed

1939 – 1945

World War II
- Germany occupies much of France

1992

France signs the Maastricht Treaty creating the European Union

2002

The Euro replaces the Franc

SOPHISTICATED CUISINE

The French pride themselves on their cuisine. Rich soil provides abundant grains, fruits and vegetables. Mealtimes are important and seen as a time to relax, savour food and enjoy the company of others. The French eat a wide variety of foods, preferring fresh ingredients.

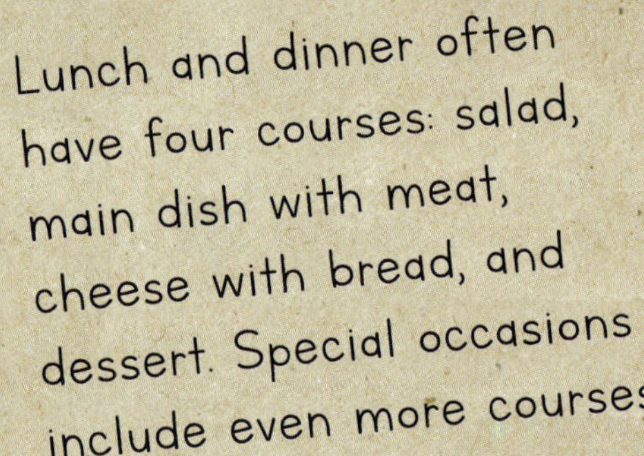

Lunch and dinner often have four courses: salad, main dish with meat, cheese with bread, and dessert. Special occasions include even more courses.

The National Dish

Pot-Au-Feu is a rich, hearty stew of vegetables, meat and herbs boiled in broth. Traditionally it is served in courses. Served with condiments and bread, this dish is well loved throughout the country.

ON THE MENU

There are many French foods that have become popular all around the world. Delicious confectioneries such as macarons, and pastries and breads such as the baguette and the croissant, are now popular everywhere.

Some French foods are more unusual. Would you try any of these?

Escargots are edible land snails. They are often cooked with herb butter, commonly called escargots à la bourguignonne.

Frogs legs are a delicacy, skinned and then soaked in cold water, salt water, or milk before being cooked. They are cooked in a number of ways, including being sautéed.

Angue de boeuf is cow's tongue, cooked in a way that apparently melts in your mouth rather than the cow's mouth, where it belongs!

Keep it a Secret!

The croissant is originally from Austria, but don't tell the French that - they have well and truly claimed this flaky pastry as their own.

GEOGRAPHY AND CLIMATE

France is the largest European country after Russia. It has an area of 551,000 square kilometres, and due to its six-sided shape is sometimes referred to as 'l'hexagone'. France is geographically diverse, from soaring mountains to flat, fertile plains.

Coasts and Rivers

France has 3,428 kilometres of coastline, from rugged cliffs along the English Channel to beach resort areas along the Mediterranean Coast, to the coasts along the North Sea and the Atlantic Ocean.

There are also over 6,700 kilometres of rivers and canals. Many towns and villages are located along the rivers. The rivers Seine and Rhone are two of the most used waterways. They are also used to produce power. Hydropower accounts for almost 20 per cent of energy production.

Fast Fact

The longest river in France is the Loire at 1,020 kilometres in length.

Mont Blanc

FRENCH ALPS

Mountains

There are five main mountain ranges. The French Alps run along the borders between France and Switzerland and Italy. Europe's highest mountain, Mont Blanc, soars over the stunning French Alps. The whole region is famous for is valleys, pine forests, sparkling lakes and waterfalls. It boasts some of the most beautiful summer hiking trails in Europe. In winter, visitors flock to ski resorts such as Chamonix, Tignes, Val d'Isère, Meribel, Courchevel and Val Thorens.

Climate

Climate varies depending on the region. The warmest temperatures are in the south and the coldest region is the Alps. The northwest can be mild and damp, while summer on the Mediterranean coast is hot.

Cote d'Azur

SOUTHEASTERN FRANCE

Pink Flamingo

Wildlife

France has a diverse array of wildlife. Many of the animals are common with other parts of Western Europe, such as wild horses, foxes, badgers, beavers, wading birds and wild boar. Brown bears, wolves and lynx live in the Alps

THE CITY OF LIGHT

France is the most visited country in the world and nowhere is more popular than the country's capital, Paris.

The Eiffel Tower

The Eiffel Tower is the most famous landmark in Paris, and one of the most recognised sites in the world. It was built between 1887 and 1889 for the World Fair, marking the 100 year anniversary of the French Revolution. Latticed wrought iron was used to construct the tower, which was progressive and controversial at the time. The tower is held together by 2.5 million rivets.

The Eiffel Tower is 324 metres tall, including the 24 metre antenna on the top. It has 1,710 stairs, 108 storeys and two elevators. Visitors are only allowed up as high as the first platform.

Don't Look Down!

There is a transparent floor on the first platform, 57 metres above the ground. How would you feel walking over Paris this way?

Arc de Triomphe

The construction of the Arc de Triomphe was ordered in 1806 by Napoleon, the French Emperor, to honour his army. It took 30 years to complete and stands 50 meters in height.

Notre Dame Cathedral

Notre Dame is a medieval Catholic cathedral, considered to be one of the world's finest examples of French Gothic architecture. Construction began in 1160 and was completed around 1260, although it has been renovated and modified since. The largest bell is known as the Emmanuel Bell and weighs 12,700 kilos. It is rung to mark the hours each day and on special occasions.

There are hundreds of chimeras and gargoyles on Notre Dame. They were designed to carry water away from the roof, but also helped scare the locals into going to church regularly.

Approximately 13 million people visit Notre Dame every year, making it more popular than the Eiffel Tower. In April 2019, a fire gutted the cathedral. Donations poured in from all over the world to restore it.

The Louvre

The world's most famous museum has gone through a number of incarnations in its time. Built by Philip II in 1190 as a fortress, parts of this fortress are still visible in the crypt. It was reconstructed in the sixteenth century to serve as a royal palace. The museum opened after the French Revolution, on August 10, 1793 with an exhibition of 537 paintings. Today, the Louvre holds over 380,000 pieces, including important works such as **The Mona Lisa** and **The Venus de Milo**.

ELSEWHERE IN FRANCE

Mont Saint Michel

Mont Saint Michel rises dramatically out of the sea, off the coast of Normandy. This rocky island has a Benedictine abbey perched on its summit, along with a cluster of other monastic buildings dating back to medieval times. Mont Saint Michel and its bay is a UNESCO Heritage Site.

The Chartres Cathedral

Another magnificent example of French Gothic Architecture, and the best-preserved example of Gothic style architecture in Europe, is Chartres Cathedral. Built between 1194 and 1220, today it is both a place of pilgrimage and a major tourist attraction. It was listed as a UNESCO World Heritage Site in 1979.

A replica of the cave, called Lascaux II, has been built for visitors to view exact reproductions of the original, without harming the Palaeolithic art.

Lascaux Cave

One of France's most famous sites is Lascaux Cave in the Vézère Valley of the Dordogne region in southwestern France. Over 600 paintings, mostly of animals, cover the inside of the cave. Lascaux was added to the UNESCO World Heritage list in 1979, along with other prehistoric sites in its proximity. A replica of the cave, called Lascaux II, has been built for visitors to view exact reproductions of the original, without harming the Palaeolithic art.

Mont Blanc and the Alps

Europe's highest mountain, Mont Blanc, soars over the stunning French Alps. The whole region is famous for its valleys, pine forests, sparkling lakes and waterfalls. It boasts some of the most beautiful summer hiking trails in Europe. In winter, visitors flock to ski resorts such as Chamonix, Tignes, Val d'Isère, Meribel, Courchevel and Val Thorens.

TRANSPORT

France is home to car manufacturers such as Citroën, Peugeot and Renault. Around ten per cent of the working population is employed directly or indirectly in the automobile industry.

More recently, France has become a leader in electric car manufacturing.

France has the second largest railway network in Europe, with a total of 29,901 kilometres of railway. The first rail line in the country opened in 1827. The TGV high-speed rail service operates throughout France.

Thomé de Gamond's plan of 1856 for a cross-Channel link

The Channel Tunnel

The idea for a tunnel linking Britain and France was first mentioned in 1802, but it wasn't until 1994 that it became a reality, with the tunnel opening after seven years of construction. The speed limit for trains through the tunnel is 160 kilometres per hour.

FLAG AND SYMBOLS

The national flag consists of three equal vertical bands in red, white and blue. Known as *Le drapeau tricolore* or *Tricolour*, the three colours have come to represent *liberté, égalité and fraternité* (liberty, equality and fraternity). The Tricolour was the flag carried during the French Revolution, when the army stormed the Bastille palace on July 14, 1789.

National Flower

France's national flower is the lily.

National Anthem

La Marseillaise is the national anthem of France.

National Animal

France's national animal is the Gallic Rooster.

GLOSSARY

Cathedral Christian church that is the seat of a Bishop

Culture Practices, beliefs and customs of a society or people

Dialect Variation of a language unique to a region

Endangered When a species is at risk

Ethnic group People who share a common culture, language and heritage

Immigrant Person who settles in another country

Republic Country ruled by a government without a king or queen

Revolution Overthrow of a government

INDEX